<u>Holy Spirit Impact</u>

08/29/2023

Astoria

Holy Spirit
Impact

By Edna R. Williams

Legacy House Collections

Written by, Edna R. Williams, Edited by Foreword Reviews, Published by Legacy House Collections, Illustrated by Tene' Ramesar, Cover design by Antonette Santillo-Rossitto and Photography by Patrick Hazlewood.

Bible verses taken from King James Version, New International Version, and the Message bible.

Quote taken from Carte Blanche and noted within text.

Names have been changed within the book out of respect for others privacy.

ISBN: 978-1-7373330-2-9

TABLE OF CONTENTS

1. You must know who you are and act accordingly.....................................13
2. Follow God's directions...................26
3. Trust God!.....................................31
4. Move quickly................................36
5. If not now, when?............................38
6. Cut it out!.....................................43
7. His perfect will..............................49
8. Time stood still..............................53
9. Stoop life.....................................55
10. Childhood...................................57
11. I want to be perfect......................61
12. Deliverer....................................63
13. On sacrificing babies....................66
14. Beautiful, Lovely and Graceful........79
15. God given...................................82
16. Batman and Robyn.......................84
17. A miracle; I listened this time.........86
18. Declare the Word of God...............90
19. Worship- A great opportunity.........92
20. A shout out to Praise Dancers......100
21. Tears in a bottle........................103

ACKNOWLEDGEMENTS

I would like to acknowledge those who have impacted my life to write and publish my "first" book (smile). Honestly I can't think of anyone that I know who has not made an impact on my life, so I'll name a few.

Thank you, Father, Lord Jesus and Holy Spirit for loving me and choosing me.

My parents: James and Roslyn Williams, Janette Wilson and Christopher Gowan.

My children: Tene', Amber, Elijah, David, Ladorn, Albert, Mark, Dania, Enoch, Nya, Tremaine, Keiko, Felicia, Christine, Martine, Nadia, Mikey, Kristen, Sariah, Cheyenne, Ericky, Kevin, Manny and Miesan.

My grandchildren: Jonathan, Crisilla, Tatiana, Heaven, Jaden, Harmony, Joel, Hananiah, Maliya, Elijah, and Bryson.

My sisters: Carol, Sheryl, Sheila, Meredith, Jennel, Cleo, Gilda, Dom, Lilly, Marcie, Sol, Tanyanita, Deborah and

Edna. Meredith, I want to specially thank you for being my midwife for the entire birthing of my book; you encouraged me, set up my chapters, helped me complete my first draft, and literally sat with me as I typed.

My brothers: Big Joe, Rodney, Darren, Venis and Kelly.

All my nieces, nephews and cousins, but special mention: William (Billy), Joseph, LaShira, Faith, Jillian, Alitia, Nila, Courtney, Bernard, Joshua, Caleb, Joshua, Teana, Joy, Yeva, LaShay, Amaya, Makayla, and Da'Nava.

Dr. Ingram and Paula Hazlewood

Lewis Thompson

Anthony Stevenson

Pastor Darnell and First Lady Shelley Harper

Bishop Dr. Carlton Theophilus and First Lady Brown

Reverand Dr. Reuben and First Lady Tendai

Bishop Kenneth and First Lady Robinson

Pastor Vernita Stevens, Ministers Paul and Linda Scott

Reverand Dr. Leonard William and First Lady Chapman

Photography: Patrick Hazlewood

Graphics: Antonette Santillo-Rossitto

Diane Malloy, who told me "Just do it!"

Seed Blessing: Lisa Milner

Publisher and illustrator, Tene' Ramesar

Thank you to Legacy House Collections, for their level of professionalism in making sure this book was the best quality possible.

INTRODUCTION

I am a Christian. I am saved by my Lord and Savior, Jesus Christ.

The Lord Jesus spoke to me and told me to write a book about my life. I decided to write about experiences that had a great impact on me. I wanted to be a blessing to someone: to show them the importance of respecting, understanding and obeying God's Word; to encourage them; and hopefully to help them not make the same mistakes I made.

I still hope this book does all of those things.

However, the Lord blessed me even more than I could have imagined. About halfway through writing, I saw how the Holy Spirit was right there by my side, through everything.

We are not to quench the Holy Spirit. Holy Spirit is the third person of the trinity, and any manifestation of His gifts is not to be confused with any evil such as psychics or witchcraft. I say this because I know that some people are afraid of the Holy Spirit, but He was sent to help us.

Through the Holy Spirit, I received guidance, love, encouragement, warnings and rebuke for my life.

John 14: 15-17, 26 "If you love Me, keep My commands. 16 And I will ask the Father, and He will give you another Advocate to help you and be with you forever- 17 the Spirit of truth. The world cannot accept Him, because it neither sees Him nor knows Him. But you know Him, for He lives with you and will be in you"

26 "But the Advocate, the Holy Spirit, whom the Father will send in my name, will teach you all things and will remind you of everything I have said to you."

Through the power of the Holy Spirit working in me, the gifts of the Holy Spirit manifested whichever way He saw fit.

Here's where I messed up!

He took me out for dinner for my birthday. Afterwards he asked me, "Do you want to go back to my place for a while?"

I know I should have said no, but I found myself saying yes.

We were intimate, and of course that wasn't the only time.

That's what we did physically; let me tell you about what happened spiritually. Spiritually, we were both backslidden.

We became one flesh, married unlawfully in the spirit realm. We were now in need of repenting, running back to God. Unfortunately, we did not.

Whether its possession or oppression of demons, it's definitely not something you want.

Yes, sometimes God will shield you while urging you to repent, but why take the chance of ending up where satan is leading you?

In Acts 2:38, "the Holy Spirit is called a Gift. As I looked back over my life and saw all He has done, and what He has done through me, I agree, He is a Gift.

Acts 2:39 says, "For the Promise is unto you, and to your children and to all that are afar off, even as many as the Lord our God shall call."

Jesus told the disciples in John 16:7 He had to leave so the Holy Spirit could come. Moreover, when He came, they would receive power. The gifts of the Holy Spirit are listed in 1 Corinthians 12; Word of Wisdom, Word of Knowledge, Faith, Healing, Miracles, Prophecy, Discernment, Tongues and Interpretation.

These gifts working together with love are the most excellent way. Love is one of the fruits of the Holy Spirit. God's definition of love is beautifully spelled out in 1 Corinthians 13.

I have experienced all of these gifts in my life.

I want to also list the gifts of the Holy Spirit which are found in Galatians 5:22-23.

"But the fruit of the Spirit is love, joy, peace, forbearance, kindness, goodness, faithfulness, 23 gentleness and self-control. "Against such things there is no law."

Thank you, Father, for creating me, choosing me, and sending Your Son to die for me. Thank you, Lord Jesus, for taking a beating You didn't deserve, and sacrificing Your life for me, rising up with all power, and seating me in heavenly places with You. Thank you, Holy Spirit, for drawing me to receive this wonderful gift of salvation, coming to stand along-side me, and helping me through this Christian walk, just as the Lord Jesus said You would. I give all honor, praise and glory to the Father, Son and Holy Spirit; in Jesus' name, amen.

CHAPTER 1

Jude 1:17 "But, dear friends, remember what the apostles of our Lord Jesus Christ foretold. 18 They said to you, "in the last times there will be scoffers who will follow their own ungodly desires." 19 These are the people who divide you, who follow mere natural instincts and do not have the Spirit. 20But you, dear friends, by building yourselves up in your most holy faith and praying in the Holy Spirit, 21 keep yourselves in God's love as you wait for the mercy of our Lord Jesus Christ to bring you to eternal life. 22 Be merciful to those who doubt;

You Must Know Who You Are and Act Accordingly

In Christ, it is extremely important to know what role you play in the lives of the people you come in contact with.
Who you are and the effect you have on another person's life is very important.

In my early thirties (when I was already saved), my girlfriend introduced me to "a wonderful Christian man" named Brandon. From the first day I met him, I was interested.

I love pretty eyes, and he had "bedroom eyes" (that's what we used to call it back in the days). He was big and muscular, smooth chocolate skin, pretty teeth and a beautiful smile; whoo!

I used to have dreams of us being old, living in a big house in the country.

We went to prayer meetings together with my friend, and around that time my mother had suffered a stroke.

He used to cook for us and take her to the doctor; he did so many things I thought were so sweet.

A Prophet came to me and told me "my whole life would change, people would see me differently, and to leave this man alone"; but I didn't.

Guess what: "this man" was not the same man I first met, and I was equally responsible for the doors that had opened in the spirit realm because of our sin, and I was not the same either.

Hey, listen, you have no idea who a person was before they got saved. You have no idea what demons had control over them. That unsaved person may have been someone you would NEVER think of dating.

Brandon began to verbally and physically abuse me. He was no longer gentle and kind. I remember one day he called me a witch. Technically, I guess he was right, "disobedience is as witchcraft" 1 Sam 15:23.Three years of chaos, confusion and accusations of me being a cheat.

I finally got up the courage to break up with him, only to find out I was pregnant. I didn't tell him at first, I was struggling with whether I should secretly have an abortion or not. I knew God wouldn't like that at all. We got back together. (Ladies and gentlemen, I did not have to do that, and I shouldn't have) He didn't treat me nicely while I was pregnant. He accused me of being pregnant from another man. I was totally stressed. We broke up again.

After the baby came more abuse. He would curse me out in the street and call me a whore. My neighbors looking on. He beat me up during the Christmas season; threw me into the Christmas tree. After that, for years I couldn't stand to see a Christmas tree in my home. All of the madness ended with him being arrested on an unrelated charge. He was given a sentence of 13-16 years. The night he was arrested, the Lord came to me and said "Edna, get on your knees and pray right now for Brandon," so I did. Brandon later told me the night he was arrested he planned to shoot his way out. All of a sudden, he said he just put the guns down.

Thank you, Holy Spirit, for telling me to pray. I had been praying for God to stop him from harassing me and making my life a living hell. I never imagined him going to prison. At first, I was angry at God, but then I realized it was necessary. I prayed God would touch him to rededicate his life to Christ, change his heart, allow him and my son to have a relationship and keep him alive in prison.

After 16 years in prison, he was released. I was very afraid at first. He told me he had a lot of time to think about how he treated me. He apologized and said he had never ever put his hands on any woman before me. He said he was like a beast out of control, not recognizable to himself. He couldn't understand his behavior at all. Then he said, "I've always loved you, from the very first day I laid eyes on you. Will you marry me?" I was literally shocked; I didn't expect this. However, I was in love with him once. He did his time. I asked the Lord if he was my husband. The Lord said "No, he is not your husband." I was actually disappointed. I remembered how sweet he was before we sinned against God. I used to feel so safe with him then. He would say anyone mess with you I'm coming. "I'm coming" meant, whoever that unfortunate person was, they would not have the opportunity to mess with me again. I already knew him. I wouldn't have to get used to another man and his issues.

We were both lonely. We would go out to dinner, sometimes check out a movie. We went to see War Room. He said, "Was I as mean as that man?" I told him the truth. I said, "No, you were much meaner!" He apologized again. One night we kissed. I heard the Lord say, "What are you doing?" It was like going back in time, I guess. I eventually had to stop going out with him because we were both starting to feel like a couple. God said he wasn't my husband, so that couldn't go anywhere. It was hard at first. I didn't want to be alone again. He didn't want to be alone either, so he wasn't happy with my decision at all. I explained to him if God said he's not my husband maybe I'm holding him back from meeting someone. He said, I know you wouldn't lie and say God said something He really didn't say. I just want you to know I will never love another woman like I love you. Did you notice I'm wearing a wedding band?" I'm wearing that because I don't even want another woman approaching me. He said I've been locked up a long time these women out here today are outrageous. We laughed. In my desire to be pleasing to God and deciding to pull away from Brandon allowed him more time with our son.

They would spend hours playing chess together. Brandon would take him shopping, out to dinner and to the movies. My son would spend the night with him and Don would share with him life stories. He would make large dinners and invite our son's friends over to eat. Brandon could cook. He would also cook large dinners and invite his neighbors in for a plate of food.

Brandon died two years after his release on his fifty-eighth birthday – a blessing from the Lord.

Check this out:

The Holy Spirit draws you to come to salvation; the blood of Jesus washes and cleanses you of all unrighteousness, helps you to be a better man or woman, prepares you to meet the son or daughter He chose before time began, and then sets up the perfect time for you to meet each other. At this point, it's up to you to carry yourself as royalty. It's up to you to present yourself as a living sacrifice and be faithful to God. It's up to you to make God proud by upholding a holy courtship. I mean, He put the two of you together, so you should respect Him and honor Him by being holy as a thank you. Love is spiritual and physical. Please don't mess it up with carnal thinking like I did. How else can a man and a woman get married and become one flesh meeting each other's needs? It's better that you get married secretly while you await a grand wedding so you don't sow seeds of disobedience or witchcraft into your relationship. The seeds will one day become fruit. The devil's fruit is never good.

If you allow the Holy Spirit to walk between you during your courtship and don't sin against God, the seeds will be of the Lord and the fruit beautiful. Everyone is making a garden let it be a good one.

Galatians 6:7-8

Do not be deceived: God cannot be mocked. A man reaps what he sows. 8 Whoever sows to please their flesh, from the flesh will reap destruction; whoever sows to please the Spirit from the Spirit will reap eternal life.

Who wants destruction as a fruit in their marriage NO, THANK YOU!

I cried so hard after Brandon died. The Holy Spirit said to me "Instead of crying, you should be rejoicing. Everything you prayed for concerning Brandon, I did. He said "I kept him alive in prison for sixteen years, I changed his heart, he got saved and he had a beautiful relationship with his son. Do you know how many lives have been changed for the better as a result of your prayers and fasting? You are a powerful woman of God!"

Job 22:21-26 Message Version

Give into God, come to terms with Him and everything will turn out just fine. Let Him tell you what to do; take his Words to heart. Come back to God Almighty and He'll rebuild your life. Clean house of everything evil. Relax your grip on your money and abandon your plated luxury. God Almighty will be your treasure, more wealth than you can imagine. 26 You'll delight in God, the Mighty One, and look to him joyfully; boldly. You'll pray to him and he'll listen; he'll help you do what you've promised. You'll decide on what you want and it will happen; your life will be bathed in light. To those who feel low, you'll say chin up! Be brave! And God will save them. Yes, even the guilty will escape, escape through God's grace in your life.

This is a very powerful scripture! God answers prayer! What I prayed for was miracles, but I didn't know that they were miracles at the time.

Brandon told me while he was in prison, guys were constantly picking fights with him. They wanted to fight him because he was very muscular and had won the heavyweight championships a few times. He also had a scar on his face that looked like he had been in a serious knife fight, so they thought he was the head of a gang. He suffered two heart attacks while in there as well. God did not let him die. I'm telling you this to push you to encourage you to pray.

"NEVER GIVE UP", not on Jesus, not on your prayers, not on His perfect will for your life and not on your life and REALLY living it, not just existing!

Keep praying no matter what GOD DOES HEAR YOU!

You have authority in Christ to go boldly before the King of Kings–Carte Blanche.

Like in the movie War Room, tell satan to take his hands off your stuff, your family and your life. Bind, loose, make declarations, fast. You can fast by yourself or ask someone who supports your prayers to fast with you. Pray and ask the Lord what kind of fast He wants you to do. Also ask for His help to fulfill it. The latest one He told me to do was no sugar for six days. Considering what I was asking for, I thought it was easy. However, it wasn't. Imagine your morning coffee with no sugar. Yuck! The Holy Spirit helped me to complete the six days successfully though. As long as you're faithful to what you committed to do, God will honor it.

Today, even as I write, it's a year since Brandon's death. I miss him; the memories of when we first began. I wish I had done things God's way. I can't go back in time, but I can tell you so you don't miss out or mess up the perfect plan God has for your life.

CHAPTER 2

FOLLOW GOD'S DIRECTIONS

For I know the plans I have or you, declares the Lord, plans to prosper you and not to harm you, plans to give you hope and a future. Jeremiah 29:11

I pray in the name of Jesus that the Holy Spirit will strengthen you to be obedient to His Word and follow the perfect plan He has made for your life. In this way, you will be able to receive His blessings.

God is truly a romantic, and amazing. Honestly, you want Him to direct you in matters of the heart. Hopefully, you will seek His direction in every area.

Consider the Book of Ruth.

Boaz noticed Ruth from the very first day he saw her. She noticed how kind he was to her, a foreigner. She even asked him why was he so kind to her. She didn't know Boaz's mother Rahab was also a foreigner.

Naomi told Ruth: wash, put on perfume and your best clothes. She followed Naomi's directions to the letter. She received what God had so carefully orchestrated. Her life literally changed overnight. She was a childless widow getting leftover grain from someone's field. The very next day, she was married to one of the richest men in the country; A Kinsmen Redeemer as well. God blessed them with a son, Obed. Boaz and Ruth were able to receive these blessings the Lord had planned for them because they did things God's way. God has a perfect plan for your life too!

Could you imagine if Boaz wasn't an honorable man? When Ruth went and laid at his feet, what could have happened to her?

Always ask the Holy Spirit who a person is. He sees their heart and intentions, whether good or evil. Anyone can fool you with the right words and have you thinking they're sweet, but really, they're as wicked as they come; wolves in sheep's clothing.

ASK THE LORD!

No matter whether it's man, woman or child, I ask the Lord to show me who they are. Don't just ask though. Believe what the Lord has told you or shown you, then follow His direction.

If He says a word sounding simple to you, check it out instead of reasoning out its importance. You can google it, check the Scripture for it or the dictionary; bible or regular. If you still don't understand, pray and ask the Lord what He meant. THIS IS EXTREMELY IMPORTANT!

I just did that recently. The Holy Spirit whispered to me "DISENGAGE". When I googled it, the definition said "to break an engagement"

YES, the Holy Spirit did!

I asked Him again and again to be sure He really said that. He did!

The man I was engaged to, the anniversary of his mother's death was in a few days. I knew that was really a sensitive area for him. I said but Father you know this is the anniversary of his mother's death. The Holy Spirit said "Perfect timing." Still, I sought the advice of one of my closest friends, who is also a Christian. I'll call him Barnabas. I told him what the Lord said and about my hesitation. Barnabas said "Sis, you got to do what the Holy Spirit tells you to do, when He tells you to do it–it may be perfect timing."

Obviously, that was confirmation, so I "disengaged". I took off my ring. I made the call, since he was too far for me to get to him. It wasn't easy, but I have learned to trust the Holy Spirit. I trust Him even if it makes no sense to me, if it hurts, or He says no to something I wanted Him to say yes to.

I have not been given release to share that entire testimony, maybe in another book.

I will say God had another plan for his life and mine. We separated in peace, love and respect for one another. I pray for him to be strong and victorious in what God has planned for his life. I also believe in my heart that God's plan was better for the both of us. It brought wholeness to a broken area of his life. It helped me to realize what I really want in a relationship; before him, I just took whatever people dished out. I guess I was healed too. Amen!

CHAPTER 3

Proverbs 3:3-6 "Let love and faithfulness never leave you; bind them around your neck, write them on the tablet of your heart. 4 Then you will win favor and a good name in the sight of God and man. 5 Trust in the Lord with all your heart and lean not on your own understanding; 6 In all your ways submit to Him, and He will make your paths straight."

TRUST GOD!

There was a point in my Christian walk that something got broken inside me. I don't even know what it was. I prayed to God to please restore me. I wanted to trust Him with my life like I used to, like I did so confidently for others, I just didn't know how to get back to that place.

I decided to be purposeful about this trust issue. Besides fasting and praying, I figured paying my tithes was a way for me to show the Lord I trusted Him and He could trust me as well. I had been slacking in this area: financial struggles were my excuse.

Love goes both ways!

No one wants to be in a relationship with someone who doesn't show their love, not even God. Although He lets us know He loved us first.

This is my testimony. I used it in a play in 2017, which showcases a heated discussion between a man and a woman, who are in a relationship. Though the characters are labeled as man and woman, God showed me that this skit was actually a representation of how I felt about Him and how He truly felt about me.

This scene in the play was called:

"Love and Trust"

Woman: Where were you?

Man: Excuse Me?

Woman: You heard me! Where were you? (screaming)

Man: You know, this makes no sense! It really hurts me that you don't trust me. To know I love you so much and then you come at me crazy like this. I'm always there for you! I have your back. You see me making sure you have food to eat. I surprise you to let you know how much you mean to me, to let you know I'm listening to even the little things. Actually, I would give you anything you ask for unless I thought it would hurt you. I hate to see you cry or be disappointed. When you cry, it hurts me literally.

Everybody knows you are mine because I'm so proud we are together, I tell everybody, Yo that's me! When are you going to really get this: I LOVE YOU, (yelling) every part of you!

I know you have been abused, neglected, abandoned, cheated, on, lied to and used in the past, but I'm not that man! Can you please separate me from the rest of the crowd? I'm not like them, and I know it's hard for you to believe that because you've been hurt by so many people – I get it! That's why I'm asking you to give me a chance for real this time. Accept my love for what I show you, not for what someone told you in the past was love. That wasn't real. What I'm coming with is real, and I'm going to give you my best, just for you, focused on you. Do you understand what I'm saying? I want our love to grow. But how can it if you're afraid I'm here to hurt you or I got some motive up my sleeve to see you fail? I want your heart to be for me and to receive me. I feel like I'm jumbled up with all the other guys, and when you look at me, you're looking with eyes of fear, saying in your heart, "What is He going to do to me?"

Listen, even though I see all of that in your eyes and feel you shaking when I hold you, I'm asking you to try love again. But this time, expect it to be beautiful. Expect it to last, cause I'm not going anywhere. My love, I came after you, I sought you out, remember? It's you that I want–all of you! When I look at you, my heart feels good. I see a wife! Someone I want to share love with. I see forever!

CHAPTER 4

MOVE QUICKLY

Many years ago, I had a mandatory parent meeting at my children's school. My children were still young, so I asked a family member if they could watch them. They said "Yes".

I'm sitting in the meeting. I had maybe been there for an hour. All of a sudden I heard, "Get up, leave right now and go get your children." I knew it was God. I jumped up and left. I didn't have cab fare, so I had to take the bus.

My family member lived two blocks west of the bus stop. As I'm walking down to their house, I see two little boys walking up the street. I said to myself, "Wow, they look so young to be by themselves." As they got closer, I realized that it was my son and nephew. I was livid because they were too young to go to the store by themselves. When I got a couple of yards away from them, a man opened his car door and motioned to them to get in. Another man looked confused and asked "Do you know them?" Then the man at the door said, "Yeah, that's my little brother."

Thank you, Jesus, I was close enough to grab their hands and save them from being kidnapped, and God only knows what else.

CHAPTER 5

IF NOT NOW, WHEN?

Life goes by so fast! I'm fifty-five. My dad died when he was fifty-seven. I'm pretty sure he didn't think he would die young. I'm so happy to say he was saved before he left. Hallelujah!

If in your heart you would like to accomplish something, just do it!

Recently, God placed an amazing woman in my life. Whatever she thinks she would like to do, she does it, I'm not talking about ungodly things or being reckless. PRAY, PLAN, DO unless the Lord tells you no or not now. Again listen, don't be hard headed.

Two scenarios I want to share with you.

My ex-husband's friend gave me permission at my request to put my designs in his store window. He had two stores, one on West Eighth Street and the other in the 30's on Fifth Avenue. Both locations were excellent for showing off a new designer. This was, say, 1988 or so. I used to design and sew a lot back then: fashion shows, weddings, etc. People always complimented my designs by asking "Where did you get that from?"

I NEVER DID IT!

Fear stopped me. Who knows what could have happened if I had at least tried! Hey I'm kind of bummed out there's no emojis on here!

Next scenario:

My youngest daughter's wedding was coming up. I felt overweight, but didn't have the strength to exercise. I was suffering from fatigue. At the same time, hearing people argue all day, every day, was becoming heavy. I happened to be speaking to my little sister about it. She said "Instead of taking the bus, why don't you walk to the train station?" Then I remembered the Holy Spirit had told me a while ago: "An hour of exercise would be good to release the stress from your job". So, I began walking. It felt so refreshing. My head felt clear and the fast-paced walk actually felt good. I started, like, two or three months before the wedding. I walked in the rain, heat wave, whatever weather the day bought.

One day my daughter and I went looking for my mother-of-the-bride dress. We chose several dresses, all size fourteen. The first dress I tried was falling off me; so was the second. My daughter yelled "Ma, you don't wear a fourteen!" I was honestly shocked. She went and got twelves and tens. I very comfortably fit into a ten! Yahooey!

When I started packing for the trip, I was able to fit into clothes I had set aside for Goodwill. As I was trying on outfits, I saw my body in the mirror. I saw the definition in my thighs: my calves looked strong, my stomach was gone and my face thinned out. I could hardly believe it! I guess it's obvious I hadn't been looking at myself in the mirror at all. I lost twenty-eight lbs!

I literally cried. God did exactly what I wanted. The mother-of-the-bride dress was fire! I felt so beautiful and royal! Guess what, the dress only came in small, medium, and large, large being a size 10! It wouldn't even have been available in size fourteen. Smooches, Husband to the Husbandless! You are so thoughtful!

Did it ever occur to you that your procrastination or disobedience is holding up something you asked God for? Don't be a weapon against yourself. You definitely don't know everything. God sees and knows what you cannot see. God is a strategist. He has sent the Holy Spirit to guide us and help us follow His strategy. When He gives you direction, follow it to the letter. I mean when you hear from Him clearly and you're totally sure it's Him. His direction is to benefit you.

So, if the Holy Spirit says start walking – walk, worship me – worship, pray – pray, bless someone else – bless, wear a certain outfit or don't, write a book JUST DO IT!

CHAPTER 6

CUT IT OUT!

A Word the Lord gave me recently for the People of God.

There are some things we know are wrong, and even when the Holy Spirit prompts us to stop, we continue sinning.

"The Lord is compassionate and gracious, slow to anger, abounding in love. 9 He will not always accuse, nor will he harbor his anger forever; 10 He does not treat us as our sins deserve or repay us according to our iniquities 11 For as high as the heavens are above the earth, so great is his love for those who fear him; 12 as far as the east is from the west, so far has he removed our transgressions from us.13 As a father has compassion on his children, so the Lord has compassion on those who fear him;

Psalm 103:8-13

That is why He will warn us to turn back to Him, turn away from evil before He has to enact punishment.

He may not send you a prophet like seen in the Bible. However, you will, without a doubt, know when God is telling you to stop.

When I was backslidden, the Holy Spirit was coming at me from all different angles: sermons, movies, people, books I was reading, signs on the train, dreams

Our Abba (Father) can be very creative when He's trying to help us get back to Him safely, before it's too late.

Many years ago, the Holy Spirit was warning me to get out of a backslidden relationship. I didn't listen for a long time.

Finally, I did! One day, the man I left came to my house. He put a gun to my head and said" If I can't have you, no one can!" I closed my eyes, ready to see Jesus. (Listen, I was disobedient. I left this man. I asked God's forgiveness. If I had to die as a result of my sin, at least, spiritually, I was ready.)

He pulled the trigger, but no bullet came out. I opened my eyes. He looked like he had seen a ghost. Scared out of his mind, he ran out of my house. He never came back talking about killing me. The Holy Spirit showed him something that terrified him.

Back to the present day.

The Holy Spirit has given me words of warning to those caught in sin. I learned of His mercy through these warnings. Things many Christians would condemn a person for the Lord simply says "Turn away from your sins. I love you. I will forgive you, wash you and give you another chance."

I have given words of warning to habitual liars, thieves, drug dealers, those in backslidden relationships, adulterers, the unforgiving, troublemakers, the angry, the bitter, the mean, the abusive, those who make excuses for not coming to church, ministers, doctors, pastors and judges. I have been humbled and surprised by God's mercy, patience, compassion and love. In some of these cases, I would have thought He would have just dropped the hammer. I mean He is the righteous judge. However, He is also Abba (Father) the one who sent His Son, Jesus, to save us from our sins. Jesus really did come for times like these. We desperately need a Savior!

I will tell you that most of the men did not listen to me. Brandon was one of those who didn't listen. The Lord warned him in March. He said "If you turn back now, I'll cover you." He didn't get arrested till August. I agonized over that for a long time. Maybe I should have said it more forcefully, but the fact is he just didn't heed the warning.

If you are in a sinful state, I pray the Lord will give you the strength, courage, determination, wisdom and understanding to turn back to God or come to Him If you don't know Him. The enemy/devil comes to ROB, KILL and DESTROY. Does that sound like something you want? Basically, this is where it's going the road you are on. The devil has nothing good to offer you, no matter what it looks like or how it seems. It's only by the Lord's grace and mercy that I am alive today to share this testimony with you.

If you are ready to give your life to the Lord or be restored, let's say this prayer together:

Lord Jesus, forgive me for my sins. I believe you are the Son of God and the

Savior of the World. I believe you died on the cross for my sins. I also believe you rose again from the dead. I'm asking you to be my Lord and Savior. With your help and guidance, I will follow you all the days of my life. In Jesus' name I pray, amen.

For restoration:

Father, please forgive me. Wash me and cleanse me of all unrighteousness. Restore me, Abba, and have mercy on me. I know in your Word you said you are married to the backslider. Deliver me and set me free; in Jesus' name, amen!

CHAPTER 7

HIS PERFECT WILL

Many years ago, on a Friday afternoon, I was getting ready to catch a bus to go on a Christian retreat.

I got a call from a coworker. She said her grandniece was in a coma. The doctors had done all they could do; she was dying alert the rest of the family so they can say goodbye. The baby was a year and a half old. I prayed and so did one of my daughters. I said "What did you hear?"

She said "Victory."

I said "Amen, me too."

Before I knew it, I had grabbed my Bible and was on my way to the hospital. I say it that way because it truly was not my intention to go to the hospital, but that's how the Holy Spirit was leading me.

When we (one of my daughters came with me) arrived at Mount Sinai Hospital, about thirty family members were outside, no exaggeration. Then there were another twenty inside the first floor; talk about support!

As I was entering the hospital, the demon of fear was standing to the left of the doorway. It was as tall as the ceiling, and huge. I was not even slightly scared or intimidated because I heard "victory" When I got upstairs, my coworker introduced me as the family minister. I prayed with the family. I was then allowed entrance into the ICU. The baby had all kinds of tubes in her. I began speaking in tongues and laying my hands wherever the Holy Spirit told me to. There was great joy inside me because I knew God was going to do something miraculous, victorious. I left my Bible with the mother and told her to read scriptures over her until she is released from the hospital. I prayed with the family again and then left.

When I got outside the Holy Spirit fell on me. I began praying in tongues. I was walking from Fifth Avenue to Madison to catch a cab. However, when I reached Madison Ave, the Holy Spirit said, "Circle the hospital in prayer; many of my people are in here." So I did, in obedience.

When I got back around to the entrance I came out of, my coworker was running out. She said "They want to know who you are."

I said "Who?"

She said, "The doctors, she woke up as soon as you got on the elevator."

I just said, "Praise God!" and kept walking and praying in obedience to the Lord's direct command. I was actually totally submerged in the Spirit.

When we got back around to Madison, having made a complete circle, the Holy Spirit said "Now you can leave." I was still deep in the Spirit, praying. My daughter was afraid she wouldn't be able to get me out of the cab when we got home.

When we reached home the Holy Spirit said "Go down the street to your friend's beauty parlor and pray with her," and of course I did. I got home maybe 1:30-2:00 a.m. The Holy Spirit said to me "Now, would it have been wrong for you to go on the Christian retreat? No," He answered. "However, it was my perfect will for you to be there to pray for and be with this family to show I still perform miracles. As a result, this family, doctors and nurses know Jesus is a MIRACLE WORKER, and this night they were in awe of Him." Hallelujah!

CHAPTER 8

TIME STOOD STILL

In my early twenties I was part of a skit for Black History Month in the church I grew up in. I don't remember who I was playing. One of my friends, Cynthia, was pretending to be a Pastor who had invited famous people in Black history to her church.

As I sat in the back of the church waiting for my part, time stood still; nothing was moving. I was looking around, totally confused, like: what's going on? The Holy Spirit said to me, "Today, Cynthia is acting, but one day she really will be a pastor." Then time resumed. After service, I ran back to the choir room. I told everyone in there what I experienced and heard. It must have sounded crazy because they all burst into hysterical laughter, even the pastor.

Twenty years later, I got a call from Cynthia. She said "Edna I wanted you to be one of the first people to know. I'm going into Seminary." I cried, of course. She said, "Honestly, at the time you said it, I didn't see it. I had no idea." Maybe four years later, I attended her ordination as a reverend. I'm not sure how many years later, I received another call. She said, "Edna I'm getting my own church. I will be Pastor Cynthia Jackson (of church of the Evangel UCC in Brooklyn, NY) at the end of next month."

And so it was as the Holy Spirit said, amen!

When the Lord told me another friend of mine would be a pastor, she laughed too. It's about fifteen years later now. She is now Pastor Gilda Cruz (of God's words of grace Ministries).

CHAPTER 9

STOOP LIFE

When my children were young, I was struggling. We spent a lot of summers just hanging out on the stoop.

We owned a brownstone back then. A lot of the children from the neighborhood hung out there too.

Those times bring back very fond memories. We were family. Sometimes I would have enough for dinner or pizza. We would all pile into the minivan and drive to the pizza restaurant on 111th and Broadway. They had huge slices.

They would come to church with us, sometimes even participate in Youth

Sundays, all-night prayer and other events.

They called me Auntie or Ma. No one wanted to mess up, or at least let me find out about it. Anything they did that I thought was wrong, I would give them a lecture. They say it was hours long…I don't know.

I just want to give a shout out to all of you: love you, and I pray you're doing well, in Jesus' name.

CHAPTER 10

CHILDHOOD

Childhood for me was scary and painful.
When I think of my childhood, the words
that come to mind are fear, love, pity and
abuse.

Daily beatings, rejection and verbal
abuse was what I received from my
father. Love and pity from my mother. I
didn't know it then, but my mother wasn't
able to protect me from her husband, my
father.

I was an angry child because of how my
father treated me. I had a right to be
angry, but it was destroying me. I was
looked at as the problem child: angry,
rude, disrespectful. Actually, I was crying

out in the only way I knew that would get people' s attention – but no one understood that language. This is why I hold children so dear and have been in youth ministry most of my adult life.

As I write this, I realize I was being held guilty, although God knew I really wasn't. He knew the beatings and the abuse I was suffering. I felt guilty. I used to ask my mother, "Why am I the bad one?" through tears. "Why can't I be like my sister?" Who I understood myself to be from my father's mouth and beatings was an unbearable weight. He would often tell me, "You ain't nothing, and you're never going to be nothing." I felt I was evil. Mostly every night I would pray to God to please take me home to Him. Fear of the next beating, the next words of rejection made me not want to see another day, afraid of what it would bring.

The abuse led me to drinking. I became an alcoholic. Every day after junior high school, I would drink until I passed out. By the time my mother got home, I was sober enough for her not to know I had been drinking.

I stopped drinking at eighteen, when I found out I was pregnant with my oldest daughter. I always tell her she saved my life. Literally as soon as I found out, no alcohol passed my lips. I took being pregnant very seriously.

I remember back then, when a teenager got pregnant, people would call the baby "demon child." However, the devil can't create children, so that was a lie. Children are a blessing from the Lord. Only He can place a baby in the womb, touch it to grow and deliver it safely and alive into this world. I prayed over my baby morning and night. I also spoke to her and read the Bible to her. I also prayed for her personality – She is exactly as I prayed. God knew my loving her would stop me from wishing for death.

The doctors told me she was due May 12, 1982. In a dream a lady I didn't know walked up to me and said "Your baby is going to be born on April 24, 1982." It was a warm sunny day in the dream.

Well, my blood was showing signs of preeclampsia. My aunt, Dr. Hyacinth Davis, was a doctor at Harlem Hospital. She had me admitted on 4/23/82. I delivered my first child on April 24, 1982, at 4:52 a.m.

The Lord speaks to His people in dreams!

CHAPTER 11

I WANT TO BE PERFECT

During those years of abuse, I developed a need to be a perfectionist. I just wanted my daddy to love me. I figured if I could be perfect, he would think good things about me and stop beating me every day. The problem with that is: there is no one perfect except Jesus.

The fear of someone finding out I was nothing or horrible like my father said set deep inside me. Fear was in my heart from childhood. I was a mess for years, and it took years for me to figure out where the root came from.

Years of turning down opportunities in life and ministry. Going to functions but afraid to speak for fear of people seeing something horrible in me or what I've said. So, I eventually stopped accepting invitations or just wouldn't go.

God pulled me out by ordaining me a minister. As a minister I have to speak my thoughts in front of people. I found it funny that something the devil made me feel uncomfortable doing, God said "You're doing it."

My youngest daughter's wedding was very liberating for me. The picture on the back of this book was a candid shot taken by one of my cousins. I absolutely love this picture of myself. A photographer might say it's not perfect, but it looks perfect to me, like a piece of art. I feel like royalty and beautiful. I also like it because, as my big sister said, I "look like I have a wonderful secret." I do; I finally realize my dad was wrong about me and I'm not supposed to be perfect. Jesus died for my imperfection and weakness, and He is perfecting me unto the day of redemption.

CHAPTER 12

DELIVERER

Starting at a very young age, I had vivid prophetic dreams that would come true to the letter. As a result, my family was afraid for me to dream about them. I also had the gift of discernment. However, at that time, I didn't know these were gifts of the Holy Spirit.

I could see the evil spirits in my home. I was so scared. I would pray to God for hours before falling asleep, afraid now because of something other than my father.

My mother's family was from Guyana, South America. They used to practice Obeah. Basically, here we would call it witchcraft, but this was part of their culture, so they didn't know it. They thought it was of God; they were Christians, using the Bible scriptures for these rituals.

One night while I was praying, God told me what they were doing was not of Him and to tell them to stop doing it. I told my family. They assumed I dreamt it, so they listened. As I said earlier, my dreams always came true since I was a very young child. Therefore, to my family, this had to be a legitimate Word from the Lord.

Do you know they obeyed God? Hallelujah, that was over forty years ago!

You can't tell me God doesn't deliver. He delivered my whole family! He gave us an opportunity to serve Him the right way!

What need is there for sacrificing pigeons, doves, etc. and talking to so-called dead relatives really demons. Jesus gave the ultimate sacrifice His life! The Holy Spirit has come to guide us and tell us anything we need to know. He is the Helper, Teacher, Counselor, Protector, Rescuer, Strong tower, Lover of our souls and Friend that sticketh closer than a brother!

CHAPTER 13

ON SACRIFICING BABIES

Lo, children are a heritage of the Lord: and the fruit of the womb is His reward
Psalm 127: 3

NO! I never literally sacrificed my children. However, I did sacrifice them spiritually and emotionally.

As a Christian mother it was my duty to teach my children about their Savior, Jesus Christ. It was also my duty to live as an example to my children.

I say "sacrificing babies" because it was also my duty to protect them from evil spirits and unrighteous living.

I started off so well. A divorced mother raising five children. I took my children to church every Sunday. We were very involved in ministry. The youth in the neighborhood would also participate. I was considered the youth minister, although I had not officially been given the title. The youth were in charge of fourth Sunday. They would have a skit, praise dance, scripture or a song ready. They thoroughly enjoyed being in all-night prayer and spending the night with Jesus.

The Lord used me to witness to them, and seventeen young people got saved and were baptized.

So how is it that just four months later I found myself in a backslidden relationship? I certainly was not in my right mind. When I first met him, I heard the word "liar"

He drank around my kids and used to say very nasty and degrading things about women, but I didn't find that out until much later. I exposed my children to the spirits he carried: lying, drinking, disrespect. I began to drink again in my sinful state. I can't believe I did that.

He would bring loads of food, give me thousands of dollars, take me out to dinner frequently, buy me clothes just because, buy me flowers, which I absolutely love. All these things were detestable to God simply because he gave them to me the worst part is, I knew it!

As a Christian mother, I should have protected my children from such a man. I had been feeling so lonely. I hadn't had a man in my life in such a long time. I fell so hard. By the way, loneliness is a demonic spirit we so readily accept to be a part of human existence. Anger, fear, depression, unforgiveness: they are all sent from the devil.

I sacrificed my precious babies to have a man.

All the things I taught them and protected them from, even sending them to Christian school, all of that. Now I was sinning right in front of their innocent eyes.

I was drawn into the enemy's camp I couldn't get out. I said I loved him. He listened to me. He said I was beautiful. He did so many things for me. Remember the whisper: "liar"

God rescued me.

An Evangelist I knew, Deborah, called me out the blue one day. She said "Edna, God said to tell you He loves you."

We didn't see each other often, so she didn't know I was backslidden. When I got off the phone, I said to myself, "Well, she's off she obviously didn't hear from God."

Within the same week, someone else called and said the same thing, adding: "Read Romans 8:38-39."

"For I am convinced that neither death nor life, neither angels nor demons, neither the present not the future, nor any powers, 39 neither height nor depth, nor anything else in all creation, will be able to separate us from the love of God that is in Christ Jesus our Lord"

And…God said, "Come back to me."

Saints from all over started calling or texting me with the same message.

I remember crying in my living room, God, how did I get here in this mess? Was I sent here to be abused, lied to, betrayed, abandoned? Why are you telling me you love me? Why aren't you yelling at me, hating me? I dropped to the floor, weeping.

He answered, "No, you are to be loved and adored."

Shortly after, one of my friends, who lives in Florida, called. I'll call her Heather. She called and said "Edna, Crystal [fake name] called and said God impressed on her for you to come to a conference at her church." Crystal attended a mega church in Lithonia, Georgia.

I said, "No thanks, I'm tired of conferences."

Then Crystal sent me another message from the Lord. She said this: "God said it's a spiritual 911 for you to come to this conference. Sometimes you have to leave your geographic location for God to bless you."

I still wasn't convinced. I had been deeply wounded by a so-called prophet of God. Listen, just because someone tells you they are a prophet of the Lord doesn't mean they are, so be careful!

That same week, my oldest sister invited me to a Saturday women's brunch. I was ready to admit my sins to God. I said, "God, please help me with all of it."

The Prophetess at the brunch was a powerful woman of God. She called the women up for prayer. When she got to me, she said, "God said, 'All of it'". Her altar workers caught me as I fell to the floor under the power of the Holy Spirit.

I remember she had on camouflage attire and she said "I'm not playing with the devil I came to win." I can't remember what she spoke on, but there is a part of her sermon I will never forget:

"Listen to me; hear me! Sometimes you have to leave your geographic location for God to bless you it's like a spiritual 911!"

Well, you already know I was weeping. I realized Crystal really had heard from God concerning me. My friend Heather paid for the conference, airfare to Georgia and my hotel stay.

Every day the conference speakers dealt with an area of my life from childhood to this moment. Both Heather and Crystal said this might as well be "The Edna Williams" conference. They also said they felt the only reason they were there was to be my companions on this very important journey. God did a lifetime of healing in that conference. One evening, while in service, Heather said to me, "Edna, let's not go tomorrow for the morning service. I just want to rest." I said "OK" As soon as I said OK, the Holy Spirit said, "No, you must go to the morning session!"

At the morning session, the Man of God talked about being in backslidden relationships. All about me! Then he made this altar call: "Anyone brave enough to come and admit their sin in front of all these people, come up for prayer." I jumped up and ran to the altar a lot of people went up. He prayed over us. I remember feeling naked when I left the altar.

Later, my spiritual father said it was because of my openness and being willing to admit my sin. He smiled and said, "Remember in the beginning, with Adam and Eve." By the end of the week, I had cried a river of tears, been prayed over several times and loved on by my friends. I called the man I had been dating, I'll call him "Death." I broke up with him. He was very upset. He asked if he could still pick me up at the airport. I let him. I remember him taking me to get something to eat. I was kind of scared to eat; I feel there is something spiritual about sitting with people to eat or walking with them.

He pleaded with me to stay with him. However, by this time I had already found out the truth to another lie. He was married! So, for real, where was this going to go–no-where!

The week after I got back from Georgia, I was praying in the living room with my children. I clearly heard the Lord say "Edna, tell the devil to get out of your house!" For some reason I didn't do it.

I was on my knees. The next thing I knew I had slipped down into hell. It was dark and there was fire all around me. There were beastly figures grabbing at me.

I was screaming, "JESUS, PLEASE DON'T LEAVE ME HERE!"

My children said I was screaming "I'm going to die!" At the same time, the Lord told my cousin in Jersey, "Call Edna right now!" When she called, she could hear me screaming hysterically. She told my kids to put the phone by my ear. I could very faintly hear her saying "Edna, say, 'Greater is He that is within you than He that's in the World.'" Her voice sounded so small, like she was miles away. I tried so hard to say it, but my mouth couldn't form the words. I felt like I had a speech impairment. The more I tried, the better I got, and the louder my cousin's voice became, until finally I was in my living room again.

The Lord said to me, "I saved you so you would never have to see or be in that place. Don't ever forget that!"

I felt like someone had hit me in the head with a sledge-hammer. I could also feel a heavy demonic presence around me, almost choking me. When the Lord brought me back, I was totally shaken and my kids were scared and crying.

The next morning, I woke up to feeling that same demonic presence. I was scared, so I called my cousin. She began to say the scripture with me again and the demons left. She asked me softly, "Edna, are you living right before the Lord?" I said I wasn't, but I am now.

The Lord spoke to me after the phone call. He said "I want you to stop taking his calls. Throw out everything he ever gave you. He is not and cannot be your friend!"

The Lord was so angry! He said, "You cheated on me, but I love you. I want you back. I forgive you, but I don't want anything of his in my house."

I realized, at this point, I was His wife. Like any man, he wouldn't want any gifts in his house from an adulterous relationship.

In the trash went: brand new TV, DVD player, speakers, a down coat, a suede coat, clothes, shoes, boots, a diamond necklace and gold earrings.

As shameful as the experience was, it made me see how much God loves me.

Out of all the testimonies I have, this one means the most to me.

I think of the scripture, Isaiah 43, "I'd give up all creation for you!" (message version)

Now that's a lot of loving!

Brothers and sisters, there is no man or woman, no situation worth sacrificing your children for. None whatsoever!

CHAPTER 14

BEAUTIFUL, LOVELY AND GRACEFUL!

As I shared with you in an earlier chapter, my father was very verbally and physically abusive to me. He often told me I was nothing and would never be anything. As I write this, I realize that had to be an evil spirit, because other parents were saying that to their kids back then too.

I grew up feeling ugly, unwanted, and deserving of ill treatment. I hated what I saw in the mirror. I had no antenna! I was used to abuse, rejection, being cursed at, let down and violated. So, I didn't know what was acceptable in a relationship. I actually stayed in relationships with men that I knew I really didn't like; I didn't like the things they said or the way they treated me. Unfortunately, I didn't think I deserved better.

Crystal and I went to another conference. This time it was a prophetic conference in Atlanta, GA.

It was the purpose in my heart to carry all the people I loved to the altar with me spiritually. I wanted them to be blessed too. When I got to the altar, one of the prophets said "You come with many." I smiled to myself; God heard me. Then the other prophet began to sing a song of the Lord. All of a sudden, I started dancing. I closed my eyes and the Holy Spirit and I danced. There were at least 150 people in the room, but it felt like it was just the two of us.

In the Spirit, I saw myself in a beautiful white gown with diamonds all over it, glistening. In actuality, I had sweats on. I didn't carry enough clothes. The Prophet also said to me, "The Lord said to tell you, 'You are beautiful, lovely and graceful!'" For the rest of the weekend, people kept coming to me saying how beautiful, graceful and anointed the dance was. I felt like a celebrity.

I never forgot that experience and what the Lord said. However, I do have to remind myself some days how God sees me.

If God said it, it is so!

Therefore, I can only be around people who see and affirm me the way God does:

BEAUTIFUL, LOVELY AND GRACEFUL!

CHAPTER 15

GOD GIVEN

When I was twenty years old, I had a dream. I was on the beach. I was sitting in a circle with my oldest daughter and three other children. I couldn't see their faces or genders, but I knew they were mine. My oldest daughter was about a year old at the time. I looked over by the water. There was a light-skinned, red-headed baby girl sitting by herself. I picked her up and said "Where's your Mommy?" She looked the same age as my daughter. I looked up and down the beach. There was no one around. I took her back to my children and we all sat in the circle together. I woke up wondering what that meant. I felt it was a God dream.

About fourteen years later, I'm on a bus ride with my church. My "God-given" Daughter was laying on my lap. She had a stomach ache. I was rubbing her back. As I looked down at her, the sun was shining on her. Her red hair was glistening through the dark brown strands. I don't remember if the Lord flashed the dream before me or I just had an "aha" moment. I literally yelled, "The red-haired baby!" She jumped up because I scared her. So, I told her about the dream. She smiled and laid back down. Guess what! She and my oldest daughter were born eighteen days apart! They WERE the same age! I called them my twins. I actually dressed them alike for a while. I also had three more children, just as the dream showed me.

My God-given baby has gone on to be with the Lord. I thank God for her presence in my life. She was a blessing to so many people. She also blessed me with three beautiful grandchildren and a son-in-law.

CHAPTER 16

BATMAN AND ROBYN

There's a Christian woman at my job. We've been friends for twenty-five years. I nicknamed us Batman and Robyn. She has the gift of discernment. She can see when people are in distress, in need of deliverance or just need a prayer of encouragement. Before I go on, I just want to say "kudos" to Batman; she respects the gift the Holy Spirit has given her and is not afraid to share what the Holy Spirit has shown her. She also stays in her lane–she doesn't feel comfortable praying for people, so she sends me to do the praying.

One evening we were about to leave work. She said, "Edna, I think you need to pray with Pam [fake name]. She doesn't look right. I already told her I

would ask you to pray with her." I said
"OK."

When I began to pray with Pam, the Holy
Spirit took over. I began praying in
tongues and then saying the
interpretation. The Holy Spirit was
encouraging her. Then He started
rebuking the spirits of depression and
suicide. I was also laying hands on her as
the Spirit led me to. Afterwards, she said
to us, "My plan was to commit suicide. I
took tomorrow off to make sure no one
would be able to revive me. I heard what
the Lord said and I'm making a promise
to you both, I will not take my life."

Pam is alive and doing well, thank you,
Jesus! Thank you Holy Spirit, His gifts of
discernment, tongues and interpretation,
healing and deliverance and two willing
vessels–Batman and Robyn. Hallelujah!

CHAPTER 17

A MIRACLE; I LISTENED THIS TIME

As I told you in a previous chapter, we once owned a brownstone. We had been struggling for years as a result of my fear and disobedience to sell nine years before. I was now trying to sell the house again. It had already been maybe six months. That winter was ridiculously cold. We had a lot of ice storms. We were trying to stay warm with heaters. The forecast for one of the weeks in December was going to be in the negatives.

Let me go back a little. In September, the Lord told me, "Edna, take out a loan from your pension, but do not touch the money" I listened!

OK, back to December. When I saw the forecast, I said to myself, we are going to freeze to death. So, I rented a room for a week at the Aloft Hotel on 124th and 8th Avenue. We treated that week like we were on vacation. We ate at restaurants, went to the movies, etc., while still going to work and school.

One day during that week, I got a call from my youngest son. He told me, "Mom, I went home to get something. We have a flood in the house from the third floor all the way downstairs." I almost collapsed in the street. Thank God my friend "Batman" was with me. She practically carried me home. I could barely walk. When I walked in the house and saw the water and damage, I started screaming. I was inconsolable. They called my Pastor. He was trying to talk to me. I felt like I was having a nervous breakdown. I fell to the ground.

My kids had never seen me like that, so they were very upset. They called my son-in-law, He said "Ma, I never saw you like this. It's going to be OK". I thought to myself, this must be how it feels when you're about to lose your mind. I felt myself going there. Batman called her building manager. He came and shut the water off. The water had been running a while, so even the basement was flooded. Batman and her friend left.

I stood in the middle of the living room. The water was about three to four inches high. I said "Let's get the water off the floor". My strength was coming back.

We started scooping the water up in bowls and whatever would hold the water. My son-in-law was taking a comforter laying it on the floor and he actually had the strength to wring the water out. We had been standing in the water maybe a half an hour. I bent down and saw two extension cords plugged into each other. I ran to the next room to see if it was plugged in—it was!! I pulled it out the outlet. In shock, I walked back to the living room. Everyone was staring at me, realizing we all should have been electrocuted. We all started praising Jesus, thanking Him for the miracle.

After all the water was cleared up, we went to the hotel.

I lay in the bed thinking about what got us here. I began to cry. So much had happened that day, my emotions were spent. God knew this would happen. If I had spent the money, we wouldn't have already had a hotel room. We never lived in that house again. After staying at the hotel for a month, we were separated. We lived in different people's homes. I'm very grateful that they opened their homes to us. Thank you all so much for your hospitality. May the Lord Jesus bless you mightily for your kindness and sacrifice.

CHAPTER 18

DECLARE THE WORD OF GOD

My cousin Bobby had been diagnosed with terminal back cancer. He was in the hospital paralyzed and given three weeks to live. My cousin from Jersey and her church, Victory Christian Center, (Pastor Vernita Stevens) went and prayed for him. They told him, "Don't confess that you have cancer, instead declare 'By His stripes I'm healed.'"

One night I dreamt I went into Bobby's hospital room. I laid hands on his back.

A bright light went through my hands onto his back and filled the room.

Two days later my cousin from Jersey called. She said, "You are never going to guess this!"

I said, "Yes, I am! Bobby's healed!"

She yelled, "Yes! But how did you know? Did he call you?"

I said, "Nope! Then I told her the dream." She said, "Hallelujah!"

I don't think my dream healed him. I believe prayer and the laying on of hands released a miracle. I believe the Holy Spirit was sharing with me what was going to happen.

Bobby lived another fifteen years. Like Hezekiah, right! By the way, He walked out the hospital–go Jesus!

CHAPTER 19

WORSHIP - A GREAT OPPORTUNITY

When I'm worshipping, I'm like a woman in love with the best man she's ever met. I'm thinking only of Him. Whether I'm home by myself or leading worship in Church or as a part of corporate worship with someone else leading, I'm thinking of Him, my Lord and Savior, Abba (Father), or the Holy Spirit. I think of all the wonderful things the Lord has done for me. I think of how He chose me, how He thinks I'm special, even worth dying for. I publicly love on Him. This is real intimacy—synonyms for intimate: devoted, truehearted, trustworthy, loyal, dependable, obedient. I don't care who sees.

In a moment when you want to express love to a man (or woman, if you're a man), you are thinking only about them. A smile comes on your face without you even being aware. You light up! You think of the wonderful moments you have already shared, all the things he has done or said to show his love, concern or support of you. You know him, his voice, the smell of his cologne, his laugh. Something as simple as a touch of your hand is special, or the way he looks at you.

His response causes me to cry for the joy I feel. I can't help it—that's what His touch does to me. At that point, I may bow, kneel, lift my hands, leap, jump, dance, lay prostrate or sometimes I just stand perfectly still so I don't disturb the moment. I often say, "Lord, please stay with us awhile." I could lay in His arms forever. I usually close my eyes when I'm leading worship. I don't want my mind on what the people are doing. I want my mind on Him. When I'm finished worshipping in this way, I feel so refreshed. Like every burden has been lifted.

Saints, in His presence is fullness of joy.

We were actually created to worship Him. He loves it and that's why satan tries to trick us not to worship Him, or think that worship isn't important.

I'm not thinking about any great work being done as I worship, but I know there is.

Countless times I have worshipped the Lord for hours then, later in the week, something happens where the Lord moves miraculously.

One such time was when my youngest son almost got hit by a train.

It was Saturday, December 28, 2018. I was watching the movie Annie (the one with Jamie Foxx in it). The Lord said to me, "The same way Mr. Stacks is staring at Annie in wonder, awe and pride as she sings is the same way I'm looking at you when you sing." The song she was singing is called "Opportunity." Then the Lord told me "I HAVE GIVEN YOU A GREAT OPPORTUNITY TO SPEAK ON MY BEHALF through preaching, singing, dancing, acting, testifying, writing…"

Wow, it hit me like a ton of bricks! Everyone was not chosen. Somehow the word opportunity put my salvation, my gifts in a new light. Opportunity tells me this is my chance. You may not get another one. The Lord is saying, "I chose you to make a difference!"

I couldn't stop crying and worshipping for hours. I was so grateful for what the Lord had shared with me. As I told you, God has often done something miraculous when I have worshipped Him for hours. Four days later, my youngest son fell on the train tracks. He had been drinking on New Year's Eve. He got up to catch the train. The next thing he knew, he was waking up to see himself falling in the tracks. He fell chest first. The blow knocked the wind out of him and he couldn't move. He rolled over on his back and just lay on the tracks. Two people I will never be able to thank helped save his life: an Indian man (I'll call him Mercy) and a Hispanic woman (I'll call her Grace). (One of my sisters said "a dad and a mom.")

The train was coming. My son could see the lights, but he still didn't move. Then Mercy and Grace started yelling "Get up, son, get up, the train is coming!" Their yelling motivated him to get up.

He tried to jump up. The first time he couldn't make it. Grace was screaming and trembling.

At this point the train conductor started blowing the horn, warning him to get off the tracks.

The second jump, he got one leg onto the platform. My two heroes pulled him the rest of the way onto the platform. The train roared into the station. The conductor just stared at my son as he rolled by, probably in shock.

Grace had called 911 when he first fell. Before you knew it, the police and ambulance were there. My son was refusing to go to the hospital. He didn't realize he had a gash in his hand and blood on his clothes (he was still inebriated). One of the officers told him, "Look, son, we can either do this the easy way or the hard way, but you are definitely going to the hospital!" My son decided to do it the easy way.

We found out from his girlfriend he was in the hospital. She had to actually find my oldest son on Facebook. My niece all the way in Texas found what hospital he was in. Check this out: he was under the wrong name! God was with us all the way. The Lord knew I couldn't take worrying about him. I had already called three hospitals when my niece let the family know where he was. I told my son, "The Lord wants you to know without a doubt He gave you another chance/opportunity at life. Please show the Lord your gratitude by trying the best you can to live as a good Christian young man."

You know what, I had no idea my son would be literally facing death in four days as I worshipped the Lord for hours. I'm just so grateful miracles were released I wasn't even aware of.

One of the greatest tricks of the enemy, as I stated before, is to make people believe worship is just a bunch of songs or they can come to church after worship—both huge lies. Another trick or lie is that we have so much time to get things right with God. Lately, so many people I didn't expect to die right now have been dying, mostly young people.

2 Corinthians 6:1-2 NLT version

"As God's partners, we beg you not to accept this marvelous gift of God's kindness and then ignore it. 2 For God says, "At just the right time, I heard you. On the day of salvation, I helped you."

Indeed, the "right time" is now. Today is the day of salvation.

Jesus tells the Samaritan this:

Yet a time is coming and has now come when the true worshipers will worship the Father in the Spirit and in truth, for they are the kind of worshipers the Father seeks. 24 God is Spirit, and his worshipers must worship in the Spirit and in truth. John 4:23-24

CHAPTER 20

A SHOUT OUT TO PRAISE DANCERS

One night I had a dream. I was in Heaven. I walked up white stairs. At the top there was a sea of people dancing in white before the throne. There was a spot left for me. I began to dance with them. After that dream, the Holy Spirit would say "Go dance before me," or sometimes the Holy Spirit would come upon me and dance through me. This is a beautiful experience. He is in total control of your body. At one time it happened so frequently I would purposefully wear long flowy skirts, pants and blouses I could bend over in without exposing myself, in case I ended up kneeling, laying prostrate, spinning or leaping.

I often keep my eyes closed because I don't want to see the expression on people's faces. When I feel the anointing lift, I back up or sit down. I try really hard not to quench the Spirit, although I have in the past, and I felt horrible after.

One time I was visiting my friend in Florida. We went to her service. The Holy Spirit said "Go dance before me." I was afraid. I didn't go. I told her after service. She said "Aww, Pastor (Darnell Harper, of New Covenant Temple, in New York, NY) was just praying for that." I would have been an answer to a prayer, but I didn't trust the One who knows all things, ugh!

Sometimes people don't understand it's a move of the Holy Spirit. They will stop the flow by speaking or stopping the music. Most times when people do that, I've found the Consuming Fire will not be quenched. Someone else will start shabaching (loudly praising God) or leaping in the Spirit until the Holy Spirit is finished and the Glory has lifted.

However, the Lord does all things in decency and in order. On occasion, I have turned away from the congregation and quietly said "Jesus" a few times to come out of the Spirit.

If you are serious about the praise dance ministry, God will anoint you and take you to higher levels. In the Old Testament, the singers and dancers went ahead of the soldiers in times of battle. Great spiritual wars are won in dance, and the devil knows that. This is not a ministry to play with or be in just to be seen.

CHAPTER 21

TEARS IN A BOTTLE

Psalm 56:8-9

"8Thou tellest my wanderings: put thou my tears into thy bottle: are they not in thy book? 9 When I cry unto thee, then shall mine enemies turn back: this I know; for God is for me."

The Lord spoke to me about all my children.

I also dreamt about my youngest daughter's arrival and my niece. In the dream, it was a rainy day. I was holding a full-size baby, light skinned (my niece). Then I crossed the street; I was outside with my father. My baby was in a light-blue rectangular box with no clothes on. I kept trying to cover the baby but couldn't.

My dad said, "So this is supposed to be my grandson, huh?" We went into the house. I was in my room looking in the closet. There were only a few clothes for the baby. Then I woke up.

Well, my baby was born premature. It was a girl. Back then they used to make mistakes on gender. I had a very difficult time delivering her. They tried to stop her from coming with different medications, to no avail. The doctor thought both of us were going to die. They immediately took her to the ICU. I hardly remembered what she looked like.

As soon as I could, I went to see her. I was worried because, throughout the pregnancy, doctors kept saying she was going to die. I nervously asked to see baby girl Thompson.

The nurse said, "She's our favorite!" I followed the nurse, walking past many obviously sick babies. My heart was racing. When I got to her, she was in an incubator (light-blue rectangular box!).

She couldn't be covered because the light was healing her (kept trying to cover her but couldn't). Since she was premature, I didn't have a baby shower yet and the few clothes I picked up (unisex) were way too big for her (only a few clothes!).

When I was carrying my oldest son, the Lord told me to name him Elijah. Elijah means, "Yahweh is my God!" When I was in labor, dilated 9 cm, I just couldn't take the pain anymore. I mean, I had the IV pole swinging around the bed.

It was February 13, 11:40 p.m. I really wanted him to be a Valentine's baby. I prayed, I said "God, I can't take the pain anymore. Can I push?" (God said yes)

Now, let me tell you the doctor said it would take another hour to dilate! I started pushing. The nurse was like, "What are you doing? Are you crazy? You're going to get ripped up!"

The doctor came running. When Elijah came out, he was blue. The cord was wrapped around his neck. There was no cry for, honestly, I don't know how long. It felt like hours! Finally, I heard his cry. The nurse who yelled at me turned and looked at me in amazement! Like, how did she know? In another hour, Elijah would have died.

No dreams or visions with my youngest son, but the Lord told me to let Elijah name him. He named him David, which means beloved. David was his favorite Bible character.

When I think about it, I dreamt about my niece Jillian being a girl, my niece Courtney, granddaughter Maliya, grandson Elijah, niece Grace, grandson Bryson, and according to my last dream, another girl is on the way!

Though I didn't have a dream about her, I want to mention my grandniece Joelianna, who despite the doctors words, defied all odds and is alive and well.

My Pastor (Darnell Harper of New Covenant Temple) often says, "Your testimony may be someone's medicine!"

So true! I have shared my testimonies concerning the birth and raising of my children many times. At the time I was going through it, it was very hard. Many tears! Never would I imagine that those tears would be like precious gold to someone. Even as I'm writing, I think about how the Lord holds our tears in His bottle. I wonder, what is He seeing in those tears: our faith, anguish, our trust in what He said, steadfastness, our love and belief in Him? Is that what He's writing in His book?

Weeping may endure for a night, but joy comes in the morning.

"It's morning!"

I believe Holy Spirit shares to encourage the believers and unbelievers as well. God has always desired to share Himself with us, and through the Holy Spirit He does just that.

The experiences I went through have been such a blessing in my life! I learned to depend on the Holy Spirit's guidance. If God said it, that's what it would be!

We are not to quench the Holy Spirit. Also, Holy Spirit, the third person of the trinity, is not to be confused with any evil such as psychics or witchcraft.

I'm ending here, but my life is still unfolding. I'm sure I'll have many more encounters with the Lord. I'm excited!

Hey! You be excited too; you are a part of God's master plan, and He desires to make a great impact in your life.

Jude 1:24-25 "Now unto Him who is able to keep you from falling, and to present you faultless before the presence of His glory with exceeding joy, 25 to the only wise God our savior, be glory and majesty, dominion and power, both now and ever. Amen."

The End